CW00351078

A CELEBRATION

FOREWORD BY ELEANOR BERGSTEIN

UNIVERSE

Foreword

People are always asking if this is the story of my life. I usually say no. And yet. My father was a doctor who got up in the morning and made sick people better. My husband said, watching the *Dirty Dancing* stage play in Berlin in 2010, "Maybe you did all this to see your parents dancing together again." A friend asked me how my sister Lisa was. I said, "Just because I wrote something that has a sister named Lisa how could you think I have a sister named Lisa don't you know anything about life and art and me?" "What's your sister's name?" he asked humbly, and I had to say "Frances." An "aha" moment for me.

I believe dancing connects you to the world with power and joy.

I think you have to hold your life in your hands, pick yourself off the floor, and try again and again and again.

I think, as Henry James said, the most important thing in the world is to be kind, be kind, and then again be kind.

I see a checkout clerk kneel on the ground to help an elderly man pick up his dropped coins; I see a young woman who's a public defender; a young man on a career track as an oncology researcher; a therapist who throws a red ball over and over and over to a challenged child in the hope that once she will throw it back. They are heroes—my heroes. Fight harder, pick yourself up off the floor, knock on every door for your candidate in rural Pennsylvania till your knuckles are raw.

And now I've convinced you that I'm Baby when I meant to do the opposite.

I thank you for opening this book; I thank you for caring about this story.

The night before *Dirty Dancing* opened in August 1987, I walked up and down Columbus Avenue with Emile Ardolino, our director, and Kenny Ortega, our choreographer. I had bought us yo-yos and we walked all night until dawn, up and down and up and down, saying we've been up and we've been down, and we've been up and we've been down—up and down and up and down. We were sure the next day we'd be down.

There are two key paired scenes in *Dirty Dancing*. One is when Johnny says, "I'm balancing on shit and as quick as that I could be down there again," and Baby says, "No, that's not the way it is—it doesn't have to be that way." Opposite world views. Easy.

The second one is when Baby says, "So I did it all for nothing. You can't win no matter what you do." And Johnny says, "I don't want to hear that from you… YOU can."

And that's why he comes back. He drives away and realizes he's destroyed the girl she was and turned her into himself. So he comes back to give her back to herself. And in the process of bringing her back to herself, he shows himself he's capable of being "the kinda person I wanna be."

The line that means the most to me? "Most of all I'm afraid of walking out of this room and never feeling the rest of my whole life…" This is the moment you think you can make a difference in future past or present … You have the moment in your hands when everything can change! Oh and it can, with bravery and honor … and luck.

Why did I do this?

To bring back partner dancing?

To see my parents, long gone, dancing together?

To be able to do the mambo and the Dirty Dancing steps of my girlhood and call it work?

The other night I was dancing at an Afro-Cuban club. No one knew who I was. If I'd let the bandleader announce my connection to *Dirty Dancing* the whole room would have instantly become a different place. But I didn't want it to be a different place. I wanted to be down on the floor dancing with whoever asked me when the music changed.

And what I want most of all is for you to pick up your life in your hands and run with it—attach yourself to passion, to truth, to bravery— be kind, be kind, and then again be kind. Look at people around you and see it's always harder than you think—people have their own good reasons, and even if you do things for good reasons you may fall and fail and hurt those around you and feel defeated and alone, so alone.

It all goes on and on, up and down and up and down in the dawn on Columbus Avenue.

Patrick Swayze was a very good man. He wanted to be a very good man—and he was. And he was heartrendingly loyal and l will be forever grateful.

Emile Ardolino, Jerry Orbach, Jack Weston, Honi Coles, Max Cantor... The list breaks my heart. Great artists, great men, friends. We will not see their likes again.

And still my friends, Ileen Maisel, who gave me the go ahead to do the film and got fired before we could; Girish Bhargava, who dance-edited sequences no one could have imagined; vibrant Kenny Ortega; beautiful Cynthia Rhodes who loves being a mom; Doro Bachrach, full of passion; Miranda Garrison, full of soul; David Chapman, ever brilliant; Jennifer Grey, of course; Michael Terrace, always on the two; Jimmy Ienner, without whom there would be no film.

Thanks to you all—thanks to you who are seeing this—people in Hong Kong, Sarajevo, Berlin, sometimes people who weren't born when we made it. They don't write to say, "Swell film!" They write me of the beginning of hope and the hopelessness of despair. They tell me their stories and how in the presence of our movie, something changed. They attached themselves to hope. They are letters to the film that just happened to be addressed to me. In the bliss of what could have been, I'd like to sit around a campfire—read the letters out loud to Emile, Patrick, Jennifer... they're to us but not about us. It's about them. In the presence of our movie, they sprang forward into their own truth and hope and bravery.

Beyond our wildest imaginings. Except that our imaginings were to be truthful and to make it clear that kindness was all, trying again is everything—and dancing is everything if attached to goodness.

So you may ask if this is the story of my life and I'll thank you for caring. But if this is a movie you've seen over and over, it's because in some way you're making this the story of *your* life.

And for that, I celebrate it and you. It's down and up and down in the dusk—never too high and never too low, say the athletes—but I say fight harder, go as high as you can. Take your life and your hope in your hands and run for it. Run for happiness, run for everything you dream will happen to you.

Baby will be cheering you on—and so will I.

Eleanor Bergstein

3 August 2010

That was the summer of 1963— when everybody called me Baby

and it didn't occur to me to mind.

That was before President Kennedy was shot, before the Beatles came, when I couldn't wait to join the Peace Corps, and I thought I'd never find a guy as great as my dad.

—BABY

EXT: FRONT ENTRANCE - KELLERMAN'S MOUNTAIN HOUSE - DAY

Music cue -- "Not Too Young To Get Married" - The Dixie Cups

The Houseman's blue Oldsmobile pulls up to the entrance. Cars are
pulling in and pulling out. Bellhops are rushing around frantically,
rolling clothes racks. Full wardrobes roll by -- a line of dress bags
of sequined summer cocktail dresses, boxes of fur stoles, shawls, shoe
boxes piled on the bottom rungs, twenty, thirty at a time.

                    LISA
               (from inside the car)
          Oh God, look at that! I should have brought
          the coral shoes. You told me I was taking
          too much, Ma ...

She hops out. The rest of the family follows suit -- Marjorie, smooth-
ing her skirt, Jake stretching after the long ride.

And last WE SEE scruffy sandals poke out, get tangled around themselves,
and out stumbles, Baby, literally falling over herself.

                    LISA (contd)
          The coral shoes match my dress.

                    JAKE
          This is not a tragedy. A tragedy is three
          men trapped in a mine, police dogs used in
          Birmingham ...

                    BABY
               (chiming in eagerly)
          Monks, burning themselves in protest...

                    LISA
          Butt out, Baby.

                                        (CONTINUED)

CONTD

Billy, a scrappy little kid, comes up to get the bags. Starts lifting
out Lisa's dress bags, her boxes of shoes.

                              BILLY
                 Right away, Doc, right away.

Stan comes by again pushing activities on his megaphone.

                            MARJORIE
                 It's his first vacation in six years, Max.
                 Take it easy.

                              MAX
                 Three weeks here, it'll feel like a year.

                                                      CUT TO:

EXT: GAZEBO - DAY OR LAWN

Music cue -- New substitute for La Bamba-like merengue.

A long line of Catskill guests in bathing costumes are moving their hips
to a merengue beat. The Houseman family is among them.

Penny Johnson, a pretty young German-Irish dance instructor in backless
sundress and high heels, is giving a merengue lesson.

                              STAN
                 Join the merengue class, being taught
                 by Miss Penny Johnson, formerly of the
                 Rockettes.

Oh, c'mon ladies!
God wouldn't have given you *maracas*
if He didn't want you to shake 'em!

—PENNY

INT: EMPTY ARCADE OUTSIDE DINING ROOM - EARLY EVENING

Baby, poking around in gallery outside hotel, looking at photographs.
She sees Max Kellerman with Winston Churchill and the Miss Reingolds,
the Kennedys and Max Kellerman, Jayne Mansfield, Igor Stravinsky, Joe
Louis and Max Kellerman. She hears sounds through windows or louvered
doors, whichever there are. She sees:

                                                            CUT TO:

INT: EMPTY DINING ROOM - CONTINUOUS TIME

Max is addressing the waiters. They are all clean-cut boys, with their
waiters' jackets open, have the air of somebody's son.

                          MAX
                    (waving a letter)
               Why should I get a complaint from Mrs.
               Futterman that her daughter didn't have a
               good time? Why? I shouldn't have to
               remind you this is a family place. That
               means, keep your fingers out of the water,
               keep your hair out of the soup, and keep
               the goddamn daughters happy -- all the
               daughters, even the dogs.

The boys groan. They try to avoid the dogs.

                          MAX (CONTD)
               Shlep them out to the terrace, look at the
               stars, romance them any way you have to,
               but see that ...

He is distracted by Johnny Castle, walking through, carrying some
records. Johnny, tall, dark, 21-year-old young man, moves across
the room like a Prince of the City -- energy, grace on the brink of
insolence, commanding glamour. He is wearing tight jeans and a
black t-shirt, flanked by a group of swarthy young men carrying sound
equipment with t-shirts marked "Entertainment Staff." His group is
made up of tougher looking street kids than the college boy waiters.

                          JOHNNY
                    (snapping his fingers
                    and pointing at the waiters)
               Got that, guys?

                                                       (CONTINUED)

Dance with the daughters. Teach 'em the mambo, the cha-cha, anything they pay for. That's it. That's where it ends. No funny business, no conversations, and keep your hands off!

—MAX

Are there still starving children in Europe?

—MARJORIE

Try Southeast Asia, Ma.

—BABY

CAMERA PULLS BACK TO SHOW Robbie clearing the table. He and Lisa seem to be ignoring each other, secretly waiting for the other to make the first move.

                    JAKE
          Robbie, Baby wants to send her leftover
          sour cream to Southeast Asia. Just pack
          up anything we don't finish.
                    (smiles proudly)
          Our Baby's going to change the world.

                    MAX
                    (Pulling up a chair, to Lisa)
          And what're you gonna do, Missy?

                    BABY
          Lisa's going to decorate it.

                    ROBBIE
                    (softly, removing the coffee cups)
          She already does.

As they stand up to leave, Max calls to Neil, a young spindly type with thick glasses, a few inches shorter than Baby, who joins them.

                    MAX
          I want you to meet someone, Doc. My
          grandson Neil ... goes to the Cornell
          School of Hotel Management.

Neil takes Jake's hand, pumps it enthusiastically. He smiles at everyone. Stops at Baby.

                    JAKE
          Baby's starting Mt. Holyoke in the fall.

Baby shoots him a reproachful glance. She wouldn't have expected this of him.

                                              CUT TO:

INT: PLAYHOUSE - NIGHT

The playhouse is a big wooden structure with folding chairs along the sides and tables on a raised balcony. It is the place all the guests end up after dinner for entertainment and dancing.

Tito Suarez's band is playing. Tito is the paunchy, handsome black Cuban band leader. He's been with Max for forty years ... by now he seems more Catskill than Latin.

This is our own

Tito Suarez!

—MAX

CONTD

BABY'S POV - JOHNNY

twirling Penny in an out of his arms, glides by like an apparition.
Once again WE SEE his grace. His energy on the point of threat ...
movements that part the air with their glamorous precision. All the
other dancers on the floor are instantly aware of his presence. Penny
slides under his arm -- out, in, around, under and back. He wears a
black tuxedo.

                          NEIL
          Who? Oh, them. They're the dance people.

                          BABY
          The who?

                          NEIL
          Here to keep the ... guests happy.
          A necessary evil ... well, not evil
          exactly ...
                    (beat)
          They shouldn't be showing off with each
          other -- that's not gonna sell lessons.

Johnny switches off from Penny and starts dancing with a homely, middle-
aged woman. He shows her a twirl. She's hesitant. He urges her and
shows her again. She does. She smiles up at him and suddenly looks
beautiful with pleasure.

                                                        CUT TO:

EXT: BACKWOODS PATH - NIGHT

Baby follows Johnny. He goes up a bridge and disappears up steep steps.
As the ground gets scruffier, she sees Billy, who is staggering under
the weight of a huge watermelon, about to startup the same steep flight
of wooden steps, calls out to him.

                    BILLY
          Baby, how'd you get here?

                    BABY
          I was taking a walk.

                    BILLY
          Go back.

                    BABY
          I'll help you.

She takes one end of the watermelon.

                    BILLY
          No, Baby.

                    BABY
          What's up there?

                    BILLY
          No guests allowed. House rule.

                         BILLY (CONTD)
                    (last attempt)
               Look, go back to the Playhouse, Baby.
               I saw you dancin' with the little
               bossman ...

He hums the tune they were dancing, mimics Neil's goopy
dancing with his shoulder.

Baby giggles, then looks at him speculatively. She releases
the watermelon, starts to leave.

                         BILLY
                    (sinking to his knees with the
                     extra weight)
               Can you keep a secret?

She returns, picks up her end of the watermelon, and they
start walking away.

                         BILLY (CONTD)
               Your parents would kill you ...
               Max would kill me.

But they're coming closer to the wooden staff house, music
growing more audible. On they go.

                                                  CUT TO:

INT: STAFF QUARTERS - NIGHT

Music cue -- The Contours' "Do You Love Me?" explodes on the
sound track as the door opens.

The following is a series of QUICK CUTS.

Baby's face. Her eyes open wide in shock.

                                                  CUT TO:

A pelvis grinding away. PAN TO SEE other bodies moving with
a pelvic, emotional response to the music.

                                                  CUT TO:

Baby's mouth slowly opens.

                                                  CUT TO:

Gyrating hips bumping into each other.

                                                  CUT TO:

Do you love me...
now that I can dance?

INT: STAFF QUARTERS - ENTRANCE - NIGHT

The door swings open and Johnny and Penny make an entrance.

They are dressed in their evening clothes as opposed to the jeans and sweaters around them.

As they move onto the dance floor, the other dancers pause a beat in anticipation.

Penny and Johnny stand motionless for an instant, as if to prolong the suspense, then swoop down together into a perfectly timed series of swaying maneuvers.

ANOTHER ANGLE SHOWS the others resuming their own dancing -- but Penny and Johnny's movements are easily wilder than the others, their leaps higher, their gestures more polished and striking.

Johnny slices down in a deep pivot, bounces off Penny's hip with his shoulder. This is the signal which starts it all over the room, everyone making contact with each other and bumping into everyone else with some part of their body -- elbow against ankle, shoulder against hip, wrist against waist, etc. All the dancers are working their way around the room.

Johnny is making his way toward them, bumps Billy's back with his shoulder.

                    JOHNNY
          Hey cuz, how's it going?

He stops dead when he sees it's Baby. It's real trouble to see a guest down here.

                    JOHNNY
          What's she doin' here?

                    BILLY
          She came with me. She's with me.

I carried a *watermelon.*

—BABY

"I remember when I first read the script.
I went, 'Wait, this is me; I have to do this.
I mean, this is a perfect, perfect part for me.'"

—JENNIFER GREY

CONTD

Baby approaches Penny, remembering her encouraging smile the night
before.

                    BABY
               (shyly)
          Were you really in the Rockettes?

Penny doesn't answer.

                    BABY
               (contd)
          I think you're a wonderful dancer.

                    PENNY
               (stacking the wigs determinedly)
          Yeah, well, my mother kicked me out when I
          was sixteen and I've been dancing ever
          since. It's the only thing I've ever
          wanted to do anyway.

She snaps the wig suitcase closed.

                    BABY
               (admiring her focus)
          I envy you!

                    PENNY
               (turns around and stares at her,
               slams lid down)

She rushes away. Baby's eyes fill with tears, which she brushes away
angrily.

Last month I took a girl away from Jamie, the lifeguard. And he said to her right in front of me,

"*What does he have that I don't have?*"

And she said,

"*Two hotels.*"

—NEIL

                    PENNY
                (interrupting)
            And besides, it wouldn't be enough.

He stops, stricken, shamed.

                    PENNY (CONTD)
                (begins to weep with wild
                bitterness)
            Oh God, it's hopeless!

REACTION - BABY

steps forward instinctively. She's never seen anyone so desperate.

                    BABY
            Don't say that ... there's nothing so bad
            that it can't be worked out.

                    PENNY
            Baby, that's your name? You know what,
            Baby, you don't know shit about my
            problems.

                    BILLY
            I told her.

                    PENNY
            Jesus, Billy, now she tells her little
            management boyfriend and we all get fired.
            Why not skywrite it -- "Penny got knocked
            up by Robbie the Creep."

                    BABY
                (shocked)
            Robbie?

                    JOHNNY
            I'll kill him.

                    PENNY
            He's not worth it, Johnny.

                                        (CONTINUED)

Go back to your

playpen,

Baby.

—PENNY

CONTD

Robbie pulls a book out of his back pocket.

                    ROBBIE
          Some people count and some people
          don't ... read it, Baby. I think it's a
          book you'll enjoy, but make sure you
          return it -- I have some notes in the
          margin.

CAMERA ANGLE REVEALS a dog-eared copy of The Fountainhead

Guests are starting to file into the dining room for breakfast,
including the old couple, Mr. and Mrs. Schumacher, we saw earlier. They
peer into the Danish basket to make sure they have a blueberry as well
as prune.

                    BABY
               (hissing)
          You make me sick. Stay away from me, and
          stay away from my sister -- or I'll have
          you fired.

She upends her ice water pitcher down Robbie's pants.

                    MRS. SCHUMACHER
               (holding up her empty glass)
          Oy, vill you look at that? Vater, vater
          everywhere but not a drop to drink, eh,
          boychik?

                                                        CUT TO:

EXT: GOLF PUTTING GREEN - DAY

Marjorie is putting golf balls, squatting down, squinting for the roll
of the grass. Jake is giving her suggestions - "you're missing the feel
of the grass," "you're correcting too much..."

Baby's standing next to Jake, trying to have a serious conversation.

                    BABY
          Daddy, someone is in trouble.

                    JAKE
          Besides your mother? You're not lining it
          up straight, Margie.

                                                   (CONTINUED)

You make me sick.

Stay away from me. Stay away from my sister—or I'll have you fired.

                    BABY
         And you always told me if someone was in
         trouble, I should try to help.
                   (she takes a deep breath)
         Daddy, could you lend me two hundred and
         fifty dollars?

                    JAKE
                   (turning to her with quick concern)
         Are you all right, Baby? Are you in any
         kind of trouble?

                    BABY
         No, no, it's not for me...could you lend
         it to me?

                    JAKE
         That's a lot of money, Baby, what's it
         for?

Marjorie glances over.

                    MARJORIE
         Baby, stand up straight!

Her ball misses the hole on the right.

                    BABY
                   (ignores her)
         I can't tell you.
                   (pause)
         It's hard for me to say that, but I can't
         tell you.

                    JAKE
         We always said you could tell me anything.

                    BABY
         I can't tell you this.

The ball rolls way by the left of the hole.

                    MARJORIE
         Oh no!

It's not illegal, is it?

—JAKE

No, Daddy.

—BABY

That was a stupid thing to ask. Forgive me. I'll have it for you before dinner.

—JAKE

                         BABY
         But can't someone else fill in?

                        JOHNNY
         No, miss fixit, someone else can't fill
         in. Marie's gotta work all day, can't
         learn the routines and Louise has to fill
         for Penny here ... you wanna do it? You
         wanna take time out from Simon Sez?

                         PENNY
                (to Billy)
         That could work.

                         BILLY
         Yeah, that's a swell idea.

                        JOHNNY
         What're you two talking about? NO!

                         PENNY
         Johnny, it would solve everything!

                         BABY
         No!

                        JOHNNY
         That's the dumbest idea I ever heard.
         When do I have time to teach her?

                         PENNY
         You've seen her dance. She can move.

                        JOHNNY
         She gonna learn lifts?

                         BABY
         I can't even do the merengue.

                        JOHNNY
         See, she can't do it, she can't do it
         ...

BABY'S REACTION - Now we have a different ball game. Nobody tells her
she can't do something.

                                            CUT TO:

Is this kid for real?

        —PENNY

Yeah, it takes a real saint to ask Daddy.

        —JOHNNY

INT: STAFF QUARTERS - DIRTY DANCING ROOM - DAY
CLOSE UP - BABY'S FOOT

wearing sneakers, grinding down on the instep of Johnny's foot.

                        JOHNNY (VO)
                    (groaning)
              Oh, no.

But his voice is a little pleased. He wants her to fail. The music is
the new mambo.

Johnny has just broken away from Baby.

                        JOHNNY
              You gotta start on the two. On the two!

                        BABY
              I told you I'd never done any of these
              dances ...

                        JOHNNY
              Okay, it's one two three four, one, two,
              three, four, music starts, you don't dance
              till the two, got it!

He puts a record on. It's a Latin dance number we will call Baby and
Johnny's theme. The melodic line will come out as a ballad we use later
in the score. Now Johnny holds out his arms in partner position. She
starts to move.

                        JOHNNY (contd)
              Not yet!

They begin on the second beat -- on the two.

She does it right twice in a row. She relaxes, starts again.

                        JOHNNY (contd)
                    (grabbing her by the forearms)
              NO!

She danced on the one. Shit.

Johnny moans, but looks strangely pleased. Baby looks up sharply. It
is clear he wants her to fail, agreed to go along with this to humiliate
her.

The steps aren't enough.

Feel the music.

—JOHNNY

"Jennifer just captured Baby in a way that I don't think anybody else could have." —PATRICK SWAYZE

EXT: BABY RUNNING IN THE RAIN

toward the staff quarters, toward the Dirty Dancing House.

                                                    CUT TO:

INT: STAFF QUARTERS - DIRTY DANCING ROOM - DAY - RAIN

The rain is still beating down outside the window. Even the sound of
the falling rain has reached obsessive proportions by now -- it's
getting on everybody's nerves. Johnny glances out the window irritably,
reluctantly moves back to rehearsal.

Now he's swiveling parallel to the floor about an inch above it ...
while Baby slowly guides him in a circle. As always, she is
concentrating fiercely.

                         JOHNNY
              Smooth, smooth, keep goin', watch it,
              steady.

Baby ever so slightly loses the smoothness of the beat. He falls.

                         BABY
                    (automatically)
              I'm sorry.

                         JOHNNY
                    (getting to his feet)
              You got to concentrate! You trying to
              kill me -- that your idea of fun?

                         BABY
                    (then it snaps)
              As a matter of fact, yes. We're supposed
              to do the show in two days -- I still
              don't know lifts -- I'm not sure of turns
              -- I'm doing all this to save your ass,
              and what I'd really love to do is drop you
              on it.

Unexpectedly, Johnny laughs, grabs her hand.

                         JOHNNY
              Let's get outta here.

You're wild.
—BABY

What?
—JOHNNY

You're wild.

—BABY

CONTD

BABY'S POV - She looks down, sees there's a ravine on the other side of
his log: a sheer drop onto jagged rocks way below.

He laughs.

                              BABY
                Are you crazy, you could break your neck.

                              JOHNNY
                It keeps me interested.

                              BABY
                What do you do in the winter?

                              JOHNNY
                Try to keep my balance.

Johnny goes through a set of motions.

                              BABY
                Where'd you learn to be a dancer?

                              JOHNNY
                A guy came into a luncheonette one day.
                We were all sittin' there doin'
                nothin' ... and said Arthur Murray was
                givin' a test for instructors ... if you
                passed they trained you for eight weeks,
                showed ya how to break down dances ...
                the girls' part as well as the guys'.

Baby, game, stays on the slippery logs, keeping up with him.

REACTION SHOT - JOHNNY

He likes her spirit.

                                                        CUT TO:

You know, the best place to *practice lifts* is in the water.

—JOHNNY

CONTD

ANGLE - BABY'S POV - contents of bag - fluffy sweater, knitting needles,
skeins of wool, three leather wallets, assorted clutter.

> MRS. SCHUMACHER
> Such junk, such junk.
> (to Penny)
> Benny Bernstein's Dancing School. Avenue B
> -- that's where I went. George Burns was a
> teacher.

She gathers her things, polkas out.

Penny laughs.

INT: LOCKER ROOM - CONTINUOUS TIME

Penny pulls out her pink halter evening dress, slips it over Baby's head
over her bathing suit top. Starts to fit it with pins. It is much too
big. As they stand Baby looks down, sees bathing suit under halter
dress which is open to waist. Her startled expression indicates she
realizes she'll be dancing without the suit.

> BABY
> Shoulders down, keep my head up, my frame
> locked. Stay on your toes, what if I forget
> the steps?

> PENNY
> (overlapping)
> Pull up, watch your frame and let him lead
> you.

> BABY
> I'm afraid I'm gonna get dizzy if I don't
> spot. I don't wanna fall on my face.

Penny watching her sees how hard Baby has worked. She starts pinning
under her arms, clearly trying to get herself to say something.

> BABY
> (still talking to herself)
> Don't look at my feet, keep my head up, my
> eyes open, my frame locked, tension in my
> arms and pull up - Ow!

In "pulling up," she scraped against a pin Penny has put in a sideseam.
They burst out laughing.

Such junk!

Such junk!

—MRS. SCHUMACHER

                    PENNY
         Thank you Baby.

They look at each other, embarrassed.

                    PENNY (CONTD)
         I just want you to know I don't sleep
         around ... whatever Robbie might have told
         you. And I thought he loved me -- that it
         was something special.
              (embarrassed)
         Anyway, I just wanted you to know that.

                    BABY
              (trying to change the subject)
         All I need is an alibi from Neil.

                    PENNY
         I'm so scared, Baby.

Her voice breaks.

CAMERA PULLS BACK TO SHOW Baby embracing her as Penny begins to sob.
She's awkward--over her head now.

                    BABY
         Don't worry. You'll be fine, you'll be
         fine.

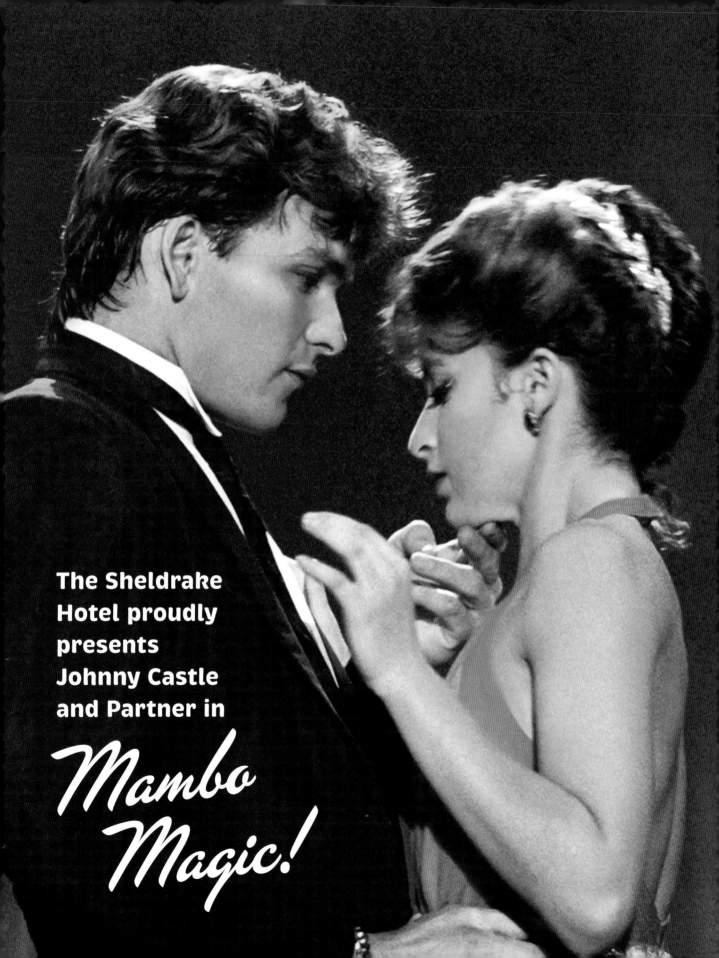

The Sheldrake
Hotel proudly
presents
Johnny Castle
and Partner in

*Mambo
Magic!*

INT: CAR - NIGHT

Baby and Johnny are driving along. Baby's in the back seat changing
into her jeans. Johnny is looking straight ahead, smiling slightly.

                         JOHNNY
               You did good. You did real good.

                         BABY
               I saw that old couple from Kellerman's
               and I thought that was it.

                         JOHNNY
               Oh, me too! Me too!

               By the second turn you really had it.

                         BABY
               But I didn't do the lift.

In her excitement, she pops up from the seat, pulling her shirt on.
Johnny quickly looks away. Doesn't want to see her in the rear view
mirror.

                         JOHNNY
                    (uncomfortably, comes out a little stiff)
               You did real good.

They drive on in silence. Baby, bewildered, a little hurt, scrambles
into the front seat.

Johnny glances over, his mood past, smiles. She smiles back. Their
smiles catch, linger.

                                                        CUT TO:

Johnny and Billy scramble up from where they've been sitting on the floor against the wall.

Billy impulsively pumps Jake's hand. Johnny holds out his, too.

                    JOHNNY
          Dr. Houseman, I don't know how to ...
          thank you, to tell you ...

Jake turns away, a quick almost imperceptible flash of contempt in his eyes.

Johnny flushes, left with his hand outstretched.

                                        CUT TO:

REACTION SHOT - BABY

coming out of Penny's room, sees it.

Johnny starts climbing to room.

                                        CUT TO:

EXT: STAFF AREA - NIGHT

Jake and Baby walking back down the steps. After a while they speak.

                    JAKE
          Was that what my money paid for?

                    BABY
          Daddy, I'm sorry. I never meant to lie to
          you ...

                    JAKE
               (interrupting)
          You're not the person I thought you were,
          Baby, and I'm not sure who you are.
               (he stops walking, turns to her)
          I don't want you to have anything to do
          with those people ... again.

                    BABY
          But can I just ...

                                        (CONTINUED)

> JAKE

Nothing. You are to have nothing to do
with any of them ever again. Ever.

He looks at Baby intently. He *really* means it. There is no doubt in
either of their minds.

> JAKE (contd)

I will not tell your mother about this.

> BABY

Daddy, I --

> JAKE

Maybe someday we'll talk about the
daughter I thought I had -- and where she
disappeared. Right now, I'm going to bed.

He walks away, without looking at her, says

> JAKE (contd)

Wash your face before your mother sees you.

Baby follows along behind. Rubs her eyes with her hand. Her fist comes
away with glitter on it.

> CUT TO:

EXT: BABY AND LISA'S CABIN - NIGHT

Baby at the door hesitating. Should she go in? No, there's something
she has to do first.

> CUT TO:

INT: JOHNNY'S CABIN - NIGHT

Johnny opens the door.

                    BABY
          Can I come in?

He backs up uncertainly, grabs a polo shirt, slips it over his head.

Baby sits down at the end of the bed, shivering. Johnny scoops up the
faded coverlet from the bed, puts it around her shoulders, starts to
turn off the phonograph with a stack of '45's on it.

                    BABY
          No, leave it on.

Johnny hastily shoves a pile of clothing off the one chair in the room,
and sits down.

Baby looks around at his room.

BABY'S POV - ATTIC CEILING

a small wooden room with a rickety bureau, broken-slatted chair.

Johnny follows her eyes.

                    JOHNNY
          I guess it's not a great room. You
          probably have a great room.

                    BABY
          It's a great room ...
                (pause)
          I'm sorry about the way my father treated
          you.

                    JOHNNY
          Your father was great. He was great ...
          the way he took care of Penny ...

                    BABY
          Yes, but I mean the way he was with you
          -- it's really me it has to do with ...
          Johnny, I came here because my father...

                    JOHNNY
               (cuts her off)
     The way he saved her. I could never do
     anything like that. That's somethin'... I
     mean, the reason people treat me like I'm
     nothin'... is... I'm nothin'.

                    BABY
     That's not true, you ... you're
     everything ...

                    JOHNNY
               (overlapping)
     You don't understand the way it is, Baby,
     for someone like me. Last month I'm
     eatin' jujubees to keep alive, and this
     month, women are stuffin' diamonds in my
     pocket.
               (pauses)
     I'm balancin' on shit, Baby -- and as
     quick as that --
               (he snaps his fingers)
     I could be down there again.

                    BABY
     No! That's not the way it is. It doesn't
     have to be that way.

I've never known anyone like you.

You look at the world and you think you can make it better. Somebody's lost you find 'em. Somebody's bleedin'—you are not scared of anything!

Me?! I'm scared of everything!

I'm scared of what I saw. I'm scared of what I did, of who I am. And most of all, I'm scared of walking out of this room and never feeling the rest of my whole life the way I feel when I'm with you!

                    STAN ON THE LOUDSPEAKER (OS)
        This is your day! Auditions for the
        annual Kellerman's Final Show beginning in
        the Blue Lounge.

Neil comes over with megaphone and posters.

                    NEIL
        So, everyone going to be in the
        show?

                    JAKE
        We're leaving on Friday ... miss the
        weekend traffic.

                  MARJORIE
        Jake, we're paid up for three more days.

                    LISA
        Daddy! And miss the show?

                    JAKE
        I said we're leaving Friday.

Marjorie looks at him astounded. Baby stares.

                    LISA
        But Daddy, I was going to sing in the
        show.

                    NEIL
          (oblivious)
        It's the big event, people come with their
        own arrangements.

                  MARJORIE
        Please, Jake. I'm not ready to go home
        yet.

Jake just stares at his breakfast, then gets to his feet.

                    JAKE
        What is it you're planning to sing, Lisa?

Lisa scrambles up in haste, runs behind Jake.

                    LISA
          (eagerly)
        "I Feel Pretty" ... or "What Do the Simple
        Folk Do?"... or "I Feel Pretty" ...

"When Jennifer and I did our screen test together, a real chemistry and a real heat happened."

—PATRICK SWAYZE

                          BABY
          Johnny?

Baby is being cut off. Her father cut her off. Now Penny is cool and
upset with her -- and worst of all -- Johnny is so cold. She's
marooned, she's no where. She has nowhere to go. She's been cut off
everywhere.

He goes off. She looks after him, starts to leave too.

                          BABY
          Johnny?

He turns around. Sees everything in her face. His face opens -- his
guard goes down for a second -- Under all the pain, confusion, hurt --
they're feeling the same thing. They're in love.

Their faces open and acknowledge it -- almost smile -- he leaves. She
takes a deep breath. That quick exchanged glance acknowledges it all.

Love is strange.

HOW DO YOU CALL YOUR

CALL YOUR

loverboy?

COME HERE,
loverboy!

INT: DANCE STUDIO - ANOTHER DAY

MUSIC CUE - "Love is strange" by Mickey and Sylvia

Door is open upstairs. Baby and Johnny are fooling around. She's
playing teaching him to do the cha cha.

Neil walks in.

                    NEIL
          Johnny?
                (sees them)
          Baby, you taking lessons?

Clearly this disconcerts him. He looks at them for a second
suspiciously. No, it's not possible. But there's still a tinge of
jealousy motivating him now.

                    NEIL
          I can teach you, kid.

They come down. Baby sits uncomfortably on the stairs between them.

                    NEIL
          Johnny, my grandfather put me in charge of
          the final show ... and I want to talk to
          you about the last dance. I'd like to
          shake things up, move with the times.

                    JOHNNY
                (eagerly)
          I got a lot of ideas. Penny and me we got
          some new routines ... and we could use
          some new music ... bring up the spot,
          see ...

                    NEIL
                (holding up his hand)
          Whoa boy.

Johnny stiffens.

                    NEIL
          You're way over your head. What I thought
          is -- you always do a mambo. Why not dance
          this year's final dance to the -- pachanga!

                    JOHNNY
                (flatly)
          Right.

                        NEIL
                (furiously, his head going up at
                Johnny's tone)
        Well you're free to do the same tired
        mambo as last year if you want, but next
        year we'll find another dance person
        who'll be only too happy to have your job.

Baby reaction. She's sure he'll blow up.

                        JOHNNY
        Sure, Neil, no problem. We'll end the
        season with the pachanga. Great idea.

                        NEIL
                (in undertone to Baby)
        He's hard to talk to sometimes, but the
        ladies seem to like him.
                (out loud)
        See that he gives you the full half-hour
        you're paying him for, kid.

                                                    CUT TO:

EXT: PATH NEAR DANCE STUDIO - LATE AFTERNOON ANGLE - JOHNNY'S FOOT

kicks a stone so savagely it skitters fifty yards ahead on the path.

CAMERA DRAWS BACK TO SHOW Baby and Johnny walking on the path. He's
furious.

                        JOHNNY
        The little wimp wouldn't know a new idea
        if it hit him in the pachanga! He wants
        some new ideas, I coulda told him some new
        ideas ...

                              BABY
          Why did you let him talk to you that way? I
          don't understand you.

                              JOHNNY
          Fight the boss man? He won't listen to
          me.

                              BABY
                    (exasperated)
          Then fight harder. Why not make him
          listen?

                              JOHNNY
                    (excitedly)
          Because I need this goddamn job lined up for
          next summer.

He strides along quickly. Baby hurries to keep up, but a little off balance.

                              JOHNNY (contd)
                    (savagely)
          My Dad calls me today with good news. He says,
          "Uncle Sal can finally get you into the union."

                              BABY
          What union?

                              JOHNNY
          The fuckin' House Painters and Plasterers
          Pennsylvania Local #179 ... at your
          service.

Then the Prince of the City turns to the Doctor's Daughter.

                              JOHNNY (contd)
          When I don't have a dance gig, I work with my
          dad ... he's a housepainter.

Clearly it has cost him something to say this.

Baby suddenly crouches, pulls at Johnny's hand. He looks down, not
understanding, thinking she's stumbled. She pulls him down roughly,
with all her strength.

                              BABY
          Shh ...

                                                    (CONTINUED)

crouched behind the hedge. Johnny looks around, sees Jake passing their
way with Lisa and Robbie. Jake throws a friendly arm around Robbie's
shoulder, then turns to Lisa.

> LISA
> I've been thinking a lot about the domino
> theory, Daddy. If Vietnam falls -- is
> China next?

Johnny, crouching down on his knees, has begun to boil. Jake and the
others pass out of sight and he and Baby get to their feet.

> BABY
> I don't think they saw us ...

> JOHNNY
> (bursting out)
> Fight harder? I don't see you fightin' so
> hard, Baby. I don't see you runnin' up to
> Daddy, tellin' him I'm your guy.

> BABY
> (startled)
> I will ... look, with my father, it's
> complicated ...

> JOHNNY
> I don't believe you. I don't think you ever
> had any intention of telling him, ever.

He strides off quickly down the path. Baby tries to catch up with him,
shocked by his tone and by the guilty realization that he's right -- it
never even occurred to her to tell her father.

He moves too swiftly for her to catch him -- and then he's gone.

CUT TO:

Baby stands near Neil, holding a clipboard. Penny sits nearby charting
the numbers on a long yellow pad.

Moe resumes his seat at the card table, with the ever-present
Schumachers, calls to Johnny.

                    MOE
          Hey, kid!

He calls Johnny over, takes a thick wallet stuffed with bills, peels one
off.

                    MOE (contd)
               (quietly)
          I'm gonna be playin' cards all weekend.
          I've got an all night game tonight. Give
          my wife some extra lessons.

ANGLE - He stuffs a hundred dollar bill in Johnny's hand.

Vivian smiles.

CAMERA ANGLE WIDENS TO SHOW Johnny standing there, holding out the
money. His face is determined.

                    JOHNNY
               (to Moe)
          I'm booked up this weekend, Mr. Pressman,
          with the show and everything. I'm not
          going to have time for anything else and
          it wouldn't be fair to take the money.

                                                            CUT TO:

REACTION SHOT - VIVIAN

Becoming furious as Johnny puts the money back into Moe's hand and
leaves.

REACTION SHOT - MOE

Thoughtful. He puts the money back in his stuffed wallet.

REACTION SHOT - BABY

smiling slightly.

CONTD

Across the room, two tables are being pushed together by busboys. Max
looks up, sees them, doesn't like what he sees.

                    MAX
          What're you doing? What're you doing?

He leaps up to go across the room and separates the tables by himself.

Marjorie and Neil start talking, Lisa between them.

Baby scoots over into Max's empty chair next to Jake.

                    BABY
          Daddy, I need your help.

                    JAKE
          I was right about those people, wasn't I?

                    BABY
          I know Johnny didn't take Moe's wallet, I
          know.

                    JAKE
          Oh, and how do you know?

                    BABY
               (hesitates)
          I can't tell you.

                    JAKE
          The last time you couldn't tell me
          something, a girl almost died.

                    LISA
          Who, who almost died?

                    BABY
          Please trust me, Daddy.

                    JAKE
          I'm sorry Baby, I can't trust you.

Max comes over munching from a basket of Danish he picked up on the way.

                    MAX
          Protein, doc, protein.

                    BABY
          Mr. Kellerman -- look, maybe it wasn't
          Johnny. Anyone could've taken it. It
          could've been ... that little old
          couple ... the Schumachers -- I *saw* her
          with a couple of wallets ...

I know Johnny didn't take the wallet. I know he didn't take it because he was in his room all night. And the reason I know is because *I was with him.*

—BABY

EXT: GAZEBO - LATE AFTERNOON

Jake is sitting alone in the gazebo.

Baby comes looking for him, sees him sitting there. For a
moment she doesn't speak, then:

                         BABY
          I told you I was telling the truth, Daddy.

He stares at her.

                         BABY (contd)
          I'm sorry I lied to you. But you lied,
          too. You told me everyone was alike and
          deserved a fair break, but you meant
          everyone who was like you. You told me
          you wanted me to change the world, make it
          better -- but you meant by becoming a
          lawyer or an economist and marrying
          someone from Harvard ...
                    (beat)
          I'm not proud of myself but I'm in this
          family, too -- and you can't keep giving
          me the silent treatment. There are a lot
          of things about me ... that aren't what
          you thought -- but if you love me you have
          to love all the things about me ... and I
          love you ... and I'm sorry I let you down.
          I'm so sorry, Daddy ...
                    (she raises her face, her voice breaking)
          But you let me down, too.

The stare at each other. This time it is Baby who turns and leaves.

CLOSE UP - JAKE'S FACE

shocked.

                                             CUT TO:

WIDE SHOT

WE SEE Jake standing alone, the mountains behind him.

                                             CUT TO:

                    JOHNNY (contd)
        Florida. They'd made a fortune here
        this summer -- hit five hotels.

                    BABY
        So then it's all right -- I knew it would
        work out.

                    JOHNNY
            (he laughs)
        They sent them off with a slap on the
        wrist and they're going to retire in New
        Mexico.

                    BABY
            (her mood shifting abruptly)
        I knew they'd have to apologize and
        then ...

                    JOHNNY
            (interrupting her harshly)
        I'm out, Baby.

Baby looks up, startled.

                    BABY
        What?

She pauses, looks into his face, sees the truth. She stares at him,
stunned.

                    BABY (contd)
        They fired you anyway because of me.

                    JOHNNY
        If I leave "quietly," I'll get my summer
        bonus.

                    BABY
        So I did it for nothing! I wrecked my
        family -- you lost your job anyway ... I
        did it for nothing!

                    JOHNNY
        No, not for nothin', Baby. No one's ever
        done anything like that for me before.

You were right, Johnny. You can't win no matter what you do.
— BABY

You listen to me, I don't want to hear that from you. You can.
— JOHNNY

Kellerman's Anthem

Kellerman's, we come together
Singing all as one.
We have shared another season's
Talent, play and fun.

Summer days will soon be over,
Soon the autumn starts,
And tonight the memories whisper
Softly in our hearts.

Join hands and hearts and voices,
Voices, hearts and hands.
At Kellerman's the friendships last long
As the mountain stands.

Daytime, nighttime, any hour
Whether rain or shine,
Games and lectures, jokes and music,
Happily combine.

Join hands and hearts and voices,
Voices, hearts and hands.
At Kellerman's the friendships last long
As the mountain stands.

Not a stress or strain is found here
For it must be said
Here at Kellerman's you gladden
Stomach, heart and head.

Join hands and hearts and voices,
Voices, hearts and hands.
At Kellerman's the friendships last long
As the mountain stands.

For our heads require value,
Stomachs fine cuisine,
But our heart needs a vacation
Where no cares are seen.

So let's join in just one last chorus
Visitors, staff and guests.
What we've shared won't be forgotten;
Old friends are the best.

Join hands and hearts and voices,
Voices, hearts and hands.
At Kellerman's the friendships last long
As the mountain stands.

CONTD

Johnny finds the Houseman family, Baby sitting apart against the wall.
He plunges down the aisle toward their seats, stepping over protesting
guests.

ANGLE - JOHNNY

in the aisle facing Jake.

> JOHNNY
> Nobody puts Baby in a corner.

People in the audience are shushing him. He ignores them.

ANGLE - STAGE

Dancers are going on uncertainly, not sure what's happening down in the
audience.

Neil runs down to see what's going on.

ANGLE - AUDIENCE

Jake opens his mouth in protest.

Johnny holds out his hand.

> JOHNNY
> C'mere, Frances.

Baby, stunned, looks at him.

Lisa's eyes are shining with excitement.

Billy can't believe what he's seeing.

Baby takes Johnny's hand. He pulls her out and down the aisle toward
the stage.

Neil -- Wow!

CUT TO:

INT: STAGE - NIGHT

Johnny on stage, holding on to Baby.

Tito's stopped playing.

(CONTINUED)

Nobody puts *Baby* in a corner.

CONTD

                    JOHNNY
          Sorry about the disruption, folks, but I
          always do the last dance of the season ...
          and this year somebody told me not to ...

Cries in the audience of "No, Johnny, no!"

REACTION SHOT - MAX

furious.

                    JOHNNY
          But here I am ... and I'm not gonna do a
          mambo ..

The audience loves this. Johnny tosses Billy a record.

                    JOHNNY (CONTD)
          I'm gonna to the dancin' I really like to
          do with a great partner -- who's not only
          a terrific dancer -- but somebody ...
          who's taught me there are people willing
          to stand up for other people no matter
          what it costs them, just because they
          think it's the right thing to do, someone
          who's taught me a lot about the kind of
          person I wanna be -- Miss Frances Houseman.

As the curtains close, we

                                                    CUT TO:

ANGLE - AUDIENCE

Jake, who's been stunned, starts to rise from his seat, angrily.

                    MARJORIE
               (grabs his arm)
          Sit down, Jake.

ANGLE - STAGE

The curtain has closed and now reopens with a flourish.

(CONTINUED)

I've had the *time of my life.*

I think she gets
this from me.

–MARJORIE

                          JAKE
          When I'm wrong, I say I'm wrong.

Two kids who grew up on the streets -- if in different generations --
face each other.

Johnny almost smiles.

Jake turns to Baby.

                          JAKE (contd)
            You looked wonderful out there.

She runs to him, they hug.

With great difficulty, he turns and leaves. He's accepting the fact
that the Baby who came up to Kellerman's as his girl is now her own
young woman and must be treated as such.

Baby looks after the retreating figure of her father -- her eyes filled
with love.

She turns back to Johnny.

CAST

BABY HOUSEMAN . . . . Jennifer Grey
JOHNNY CASTLE . . . . .Patrick Swayze
JAKE HOUSEMAN . . . . .Jerry Orbach
PENNY JOHNSON . . . . .Cynthia Rhodes
MAX KELLERMAN . . . . Jack Weston
LISA HOUSEMAN . . . . .Jane Brucker
MARJORIE HOUSEMAN . . . . .Kelly Bishop
NEIL KELLERMAN . . . . .Lonny Price
ROBBIE GOULD . . . . Max Cantor
TITO SUAREZ . . . . .Charles Honi Coles
BILLY KOSTECKI . . . . Neal Jones
MAGICIAN . . . ."Cousin Brucie" Morrow
STAN . . . . Wayne Knight
MRS. SCHUMACHER . . . . Paula Trueman
MR. SCHUMACHER . . . . .Alvin Myerovich
VIVIAN PRESSMAN . . . . .Miranda Garrison
MOE PRESSMAN . . . . .Garry Goodrow
STAFF KID . . . . .Antone Pagan
BUS BOY . . . . Tom Cannold
DIRTY DANCERS . . . . .M.R. Fletcher
                                                          Jesus Fuentes
                                                    Heather Lea Gerdes
                                                          Karen Getz
                                                 Andrew Charles Koch
                                                          D.A. Pauley
                                                      Dorian Sanchez
                                                      Jennifer Stahl
TITO'S BAND . . . . Jonathan Barnes
                                                       Dwyght Bryan
                                                         Tom Drake
                                                         John Gotz
                                                    Dwayne Malphus
                                               Dr. Clifford Watkins
STUNTS . . . . .Denise Amirante
                                                      Bill Anagnos
                                                   Norman Douglass

                SPECIAL THANKS TO JIMMY IENNER

"Patrick was a rare and beautiful combination of raw masculinity and amazing grace."

—JENNIFER GREY

"I'm really thankful for that opportunity that *Dirty Dancing* has served me as a human being. The biggest thing *Dirty Dancing* has given me in my life is gratitude."

—PATRICK SWAYZE

First published in the
United States of America in 2012 by
UNIVERSE PUBLISHING,
A Division of Rizzoli International Publications, Inc.
300 Park Avenue South
New York, NY 10010
www.rizzoliusa.com

©2012 Lions Gate Entertainment, Inc.
Dirty Dancing is a registered trademark of Lions Gate
Entertainment, Inc.

All rights reserved. No part of this publication
may be reproduced, stored in a retrieval system, or
transmitted in any form or by any means, electronic,
mechanical, photocopying, recording, or otherwise,
without prior consent of the publishers.

Foreword ©2012 by Eleanor Bergstein
All rights reserved.

2012 2013 2014 2015 / 10 9 8 7 6 5 4 3 2 1

Design by Lynne Yeamans/Lync
Printed in China.

ISBN-13: 978-0-7893-2272-2

Library of Congress Catalog Control Number: 2011935806